Top Notes

T0363052

Tom Tykwer's
# Run Lola Run
Study notes for Standard English:
**Module A**
2015-2020 HSC

Renee Carr

A
FIVE SENSES
PUBLICATION

Five Senses Education Pty Ltd
2/195 Prospect Highway
Seven Hills 2147
New South Wales
Australia

Copyright © Five Senses Education Pty Ltd 2014
First Published 2008. Second Edition 2016.

All rights reserved. Except under the conditions described
in the Copyright Act 1968 of Australia and subsequent
amendments, no part of this publication may be reproduced
stored in retrieval system or transmitted in any form or by
any means electronic, mechanical, photocopying, recording or
otherwise, without the prior permission of the copyright owner.

Carr, Renee,
Top Notes – Run Lola Run
ISBN 978-1-76032-033-1

# CONTENTS

# INTRODUCTION TO THE TOP NOTES SERIES

This series has been created to assist HSC students of English in their understanding of set texts. Top Notes are easy to read, providing analysis of issues and discussion of important ideas contained in the texts.

Particular care has been taken to ensure that students are able to examine each text in the context of the module to which it has been allocated.

## This text includes:

- Notes on the specific module and elective
- Plot summary
- Character analysis
- Setting
- Thematic concerns
- Essay question and response
- Related text suggestions
- Additional questions

I am sure you will find these Top Notes useful in your studies of English.

Bruce Pattinson
Series Editor

© Five Senses Education Pty Ltd

# THE STANDARD COURSE

This is a brief analysis of the Standard course to ensure you are completely familiar with what you are attempting in the examination. If in any doubt at all check with your teacher or the Board of Studies.

The Standard Course requires you to have studied:

- Four prescribed texts. This means four texts from the list given to your teacher by the Board of Studies.

- For each of the texts, one must come from each of the following four categories.
    - drama
    - poetry
    - prose fiction (novel usually)
    - nonfiction or media or film or multimedia texts. (Multimedia are CD ROMs, websites, etc.)

- A range of related texts of your own choosing. These are part of your Area of Study, Module A and Module C. Do not confuse these with the main set texts you are studying. This is very important.

**Paper One**

## Area of Study: Discovery

**Paper Two**

| Module A | Module B | Module C |
|---|---|---|
| *Experience through Language* | **Close Study of Text** | **Texts and Society** |
| *Electives* | • Drama | *Electives* |
| • Distinctive Voices | OR | • Exploring Interactions |
| OR | • Prose Fiction | OR |
| • Distinctively Visual | OR | • Exploring Transitions |
| | • Nonfiction, Film, Media, Multimedia | |
| | OR | |
| | • Poetry | |

You must study the Area of Study and EACH of Modules A, B and C

There are electives and texts within EACH of these modules that your school will select.

© Five Senses Education Pty Ltd

# EXPERIENCE THROUGH LANGUAGE

## ELECTIVE TWO : Distinctively Visual

The Experience through Language module demands language be the focus of study and therefore, your response. The syllabus requires a focus on how language can shape relationships and change perceptions of other people and the world. The Board says about this Module,

'This module requires students to explore the uses of a particular aspect of language. **It develops students' awareness of language and helps them understand how our perceptions of and relationships with others and the world are shaped in written, spoken and visual language'** (p.11).

You will be studying a specific text, the film, *Run Lola Run*. Consider how language is used to portray relationships within the film and to shape your perceptions. In your responses, you should always be discussing how written, spoken and visual language have been used by the composer.

The elective being studied within this module is, "Distinctly Visual". You will be studying how visual images, formed through written and spoken words and pictures, can shape meaning. Consider how composers have used images to send messages or portray meaning and themes to an audience. In many cases, composers are either sending messages or emphasising certain aspects of a character, a relationship or an event through the use of particular images. When you were younger and reading simpler texts the images would have been very obvious to you. One example is in cartoons where viewers can see the heart of a character beating in their chest as the person they love walks by. Usually this is simply emphasising the emotion that the composer wants you to notice. You may pick up the message that the character is in love simply by their body language. Through positioning, facing the character, touching the other person frequently or even simply through expressions a message can be conveyed.

In this way, a composer can portray their idea without a character having to say, "love". Just as messages and meanings are conveyed through a character's body language and facial expression when they are not saying anything, we can also are pick up meaning from these same things when they are saying something. An actor may be saying the words, "I hate him" and we are also reading body language, facial expressions and other techniques to confirm or deny this. The visual messages the audience read are just as important as what the actor is saying. In some cases, the visual meaning is more important. For example, a character may be telling another character that they do not love someone. However, the audience may read their visual language differently and therefore conclude that the character is lying. This is very important for the audience to know and is consequently why it is so important that we can all read visual images and not just focus on the spoken language of a film.

Now that you are more advanced in your reading of visual images, the messages are a little subtler. It is your job to explore what the main messages are in the film and then investigate how the images have been put together or shaped. As you have already read, a character is made up of many visual messages such as their body language, their gestures and their facial expressions, as well as spoken and written words.

© Five Senses Education Pty Ltd

Visual aspects give the audience clues about characters. Examples include the character's clothing (costume), the character's style (hair and makeup), the setting and the way all of these things have been put together, These indicate something about the character. A messy bedroom setting may suggest to the audience that this character is in a chaotic time in their life or that they are a lazy person who is not interested in looking after themself. As you live in a world where you are constantly communicating and are highly skilled in reading visuals, this is an excellent elective for you to be able to show off your skills!

Visual images 'talk' to us and give us messages. Therefore, we consider image to be a type of language. This is why you have been studying images in your junior years of school and should be familiar with the term visual literacy and film techniques. You should even have your own vocabulary for discussing images with words such as salience, vectors, foregrounding and reading paths. Specifically for film, you should be aware of camera angles, shots and so on. You should ensure you review these terms to prepare yourself for your study of this film. There are some diagrams to help you on following pages.

*Run Lola Run* is a German film which has won many awards for its excellent script and insightful commentary on life. This film has universal themes and ideas. This means that the ideas and characters in the film can be appreciated by anyone in the world. You do not have to be German to understand the meaning that the film makers are trying to portray about life. You will be watching the film either with English subtitles and/or with English dubbing. This film has also drawn international attention for its use of visual images. This is your focus for this elective and therefore an important point. The film makers have blended live footage with animated images to give the audience many different visual messages. Animated images are termed low modality images and realistic images are termed high modality images. It is an interesting, creative and innovative technique to blend these.

Structurally, the film is presented in three parts, each section showing how a small change in Lola and Manni's lives can make a large impact on how things turn out for them in the end. The play opens with a repetition of a circle motif, as seen in the ball, spiral and clock. Combined with the quotations and questions it sets itself up as a postmodern film exploring philosophical questions.

You need to ensure that as you are watching the film, you are considering your first responses to the ideas within it. Think about defining moments in your life and how decisions you have made changed your life. It is important that you reflect on your own response to the film and consider how it has changed the way you look at the decisions you make in your life. As *Run Lola Run* has themes which anyone can relate to, there is no excuse for you not to have a personal response to the film. Think about the alternative paths you could have taken in your life or near misses you may have experienced. For example, your car may have broken down on the way to an airport or you may have had to babysit for someone at the last minute which made you decide to stay at school and not become a childcare worker! Try to think about small incidents that have had a significant impact on your life. At the very least, consider how the ideas in this film have changed the way you look at those small things in life.

© Five Senses Education Pty Ltd

# STUDYING FILM

Film provides us with a source of entertainment, even escapism, on a daily basis. Although many films can be enjoyed and interpreted with little effort on our part, others operate on more than one level. As well as entertaining, they have a message for the responder. They tell us something about ourselves and our world.

In order to appreciate the messages and achieve a level of deeper understanding or interpretation, it is essential to consider how film techniques and conventions, the tools of the film-maker, have been used to make meaning. We are able to enjoy and understand films everyday because we have an implicit understanding of the basic techniques and conventions upon which a film text relies. For instance, we know that when the camera moves in on a sleeping person's face and the sound becomes distorted and echoing that we are about to see a dream sequence.

Film Study involves a critical awareness of filmic conventions and the technical language, or jargon, required to label and discuss the various components of film. The glossary included in this guide provides a basic overview of the terminology required for the study of film as text at HSC level.

It is important to consider that the construction of meaning in film is not accidental, but the result of careful planning. An individual scene in a screen-play will be made up of dozens of individual shots, edited from a much larger amount of raw film footage. In the creation of a shot, the film-maker considers five variables: shot size, framing, focus, angle and movement. These are aspects of film language that need to be considered in your analysis and which will be discussed in the analysis section of this guide.

In addition, the director uses mise-en-scene to add impact to the film. Mise-en-scène refers to everything else that happens in a shot, apart from the main action. Analysing this involves looking at elements like setting, costume, lighting and the movements of the other actors in the scene. For instance, costume can be used to convey the social status or personality of a character, lighting can be used to enhance a particular mood and the actions of the main character may contrast to those of other characters in the background of the scene. The mise-en-scène changes in the three runs and is an important part of the language of narration in this film. It warrants close study.

The use of sound in a film, including voices, sound effects and the musical score is also an essential consideration. Soundtracks in films are used in two ways. Firstly they include the sounds that we would expect to hear, such as dialogue and realistic sounds like a door closing or the noise of an approaching car. (Diegetic sounds) Secondly, the soundtrack includes sounds that are added to the film to create or suggest certain attitudes or effects – well known songs or an original score may be included to invoke a particular mood or attitude (Non-Deigetic Sounds). Exaggerated sound effects and voiceovers are other examples. Notably, silence is often used as an effective technique and must be considered as part of the soundtrack.

Finally, it is important to consider the style of the film you are studying, as certain conventions are associated with particular styles and genres of film. The introduction of characters through

© Five Senses Education Pty Ltd

use of mug shots in the opening minutes, helps to establish the element of crime in the film.

Here are some steps to follow in the study of a film:

1. Watch the film from beginning to end without interruption, preferably in one sitting.

2. Record your first impressions of the film.

3. Review each sequence of the film in relation to the module and elective rubric. Make detailed notes about how the various components of the film have been used by the film-maker.

4. Looking at your detailed notes, decide how particular film techniques are used to explore the themes of the film.

5. Create links between the film you have studied and related material. Identify similarities and/or differences in terms of the message of the text and/or the language techniques that have been used to convey this message.

6. Tie your ideas together in an extended piece of writing. Ensure you write not only in essay style.

# GENERAL GLOSSARY OF FILM TERMS

### aerial shot

A shot taken from above the scene, usually an exterior shot.

### camera angle

The position of the camera in relation to the subject. A shot may be taken from a low-angle, high-angle or eye-level. Different meanings are associated with different camera angles.

### close-up (CU)

A shot where the camera, and therefore the audience, is close to the subject e.g. when the head and shoulders of a character fill the screen.

### colour/black and white

Consider the use of alternating colour shots and black and white shots and consider their effect.

### cut

The juxtaposition and joining together of different shots, through editing, in the finished film.

© Five Senses Education Pty Ltd

### editing

The joining of shots together, by cutting and arranging, to form a sequence. Rapid editing can depict anxiety and panic.

### epic

A heroic tale, usually historical.

### establishing shot

The initial shot of a scene, usually from a distance (aerial shot, long shot) showing the viewer where the action is about to occur.

### extreme close-up

A shot where the camera is extremely close to the subject, for instance a shot of the eye of an actor only.

### extreme long-shot

A shot, usually of an exterior location, taken from a long distance. Usually panoramic.

### eye-level shot

Camera viewpoint which represents the view of an observer.

## fast motion

A shot in which time is distorted by quickening the pace of the scene.

## first person

See point of view shot.

## foreground

The part of the shot or scene closest to the viewer, often in front of the action.

## foregrounding

Bringing anything to the front, or foreground, of a scene. This gives it importance.

## genre

Common types or categories of film that are characterized by particular conventions e.g. romantic comedy, action adventure and science fiction are recognizable genres.

## insert shot

A shot inserted into a sequence of shots, during editing, to create emphasis. Usually a close-up showing detail.

© Five Senses Education Pty Ltd

## jump cut

An abrupt but deliberate transition between shots.

## long shot (LS)

A shot where the camera is a long way from the subject.

## low-angle shot

A shot where the camera is below the subject. This emphasises power and position.

## medium shot

A relatively close-up shot of a subject. For instance most of a human figure is evident.

## mise-en-scène

The various elements that make up the background of the scene. Due to overplay of scenes, this technique is worth focussing on in this film.

## montage

A series of shots, rapidly edited together to show the passing of time.

## narration

A speaking voice, either from a character on-screen or an off-screen voiceover, that provides commentary on the action or plot.

## pan

A panning shot. A shot that moves the camera to encompass the full width of a scene.

## parallel action

The use of cross-cutting to present multiple stories at the one time.

## point of view shot

A shot that shows the viewer what the character in the film sees.

## rapid cutting

A style of editing that juxtaposes short sharp scenes in a sequence.

## realism

A genre of film in which authentic locations and details are used to portray reality.

© Five Senses Education Pty Ltd

### re-establishing shot

Usually follows closer shots, allowing the viewer to recover a sense of the context of the scene.

### reverse angle-shot

After one shot the camera turns around to show the same shot from the opposite direction.

### scene

An incident in the action, composed of a series of separate but related shots.

### score

The background music, separate from the soundtrack.

### screen-play

The written version of the film, including dialogue, description of the action and, sometimes, directions for the camera.

### segue

Use of a device to link one scene to another e.g. a voiceover.

### sequence

A series of scenes.

## shot

A length of film taken without stopping.

## slow motion

A shot in which time is distorted by slowing down the action in the scene.

## sound

All recorded music, dialogue and background noise. Also the use of silence. **Diegetic sound.** Sound whose source is visible on the screen or whose source is implied to be present by the action of the film: voices of characters. sounds made by objects in the story. music represented as coming from instruments in the story space ( = source music)

## soundtrack

All of the sound recorded in a film, including the score.

## symbol

An object or event that represents something else and has meaning beyond the literal.

## voiceover

Dialogue spoken off-screen.

© Five Senses Education Pty Ltd

**wide-shot**

A shot taken from a distance, including the entire setting where the action takes place.

**zoom**

To make the subject appear to approach (zoom-in) or recede (zoom-out) from the camera/viewer.

# Run Lola Run

*"Every second of every day, you make a choice that can change your life"*

*"Cinema that interests me is cinema about openings, unresolved questions and experiments; cinema that explores the possibilities offered by narrative and by associations, without refusing chaos, chance, destiny or the unexpected." Tom Tykwer*

# SEQUENCE NAMES

There are no specific scene names provided by the composers of the film. However, the scene names below should be very obvious and will be used throughout this text.

### The Opening Sequence

Sequence 1. The Telephone Conversation

Sequence 2. The First Run

Sequence 3. The Supermarket Robbery

Sequence 4: The Shooting Sequence

Sequence 5: The Second Run

Sequence 6: The Bank Robbery

Sequence 7: The Ambulance Sequence

Sequence 8: The Third Run

Sequence 9: Lola's father's office

Sequence 10: The Casino

© Five Senses Education Pty Ltd

# CHARACTER AND CAST NAMES

**RUN LOLA RUN**
**(80 minutes)**
**Rated M**


Franka Potente as Lola

Moritz Bleibtreu as Manni

Herbert Knaup as Papa

Nina Petri as Frau Hansen

Armin Rohde as Herr Schuster

Joachim Król as Norbert von Au

Ludger Pistor as Herr Meier

Suzanne von Borsody as Frau Jäger

Sebastian Schipper as Mike

Julia Lindig as Doris

Lars Rudolph as Herr Kruse

Ute Lubosch as Mama

Hans Paetsch as Narrator

# THE WRITER AND DIRECTOR – TOM TYKWER

Tom Twyker was born in 1965 in Wuppertal, Germany. He was interested in film from a very young age and was first inspired by watching, *Peter Pan*. He followed his dream taking jobs as an usher in a local cinema and a projectionist when he was older. Another film he credits as inspiring him at a young age was, *King Kong*. He felt empowered and inspired to compose his own stories. Tykwer failed to make it into film school when he left school but continued to take jobs in the industry so he could follow his passion for film. When he went on a trip to Berlin, he realized that film was a central aspect to the culture and widely appreciated. He decided to move to Berlin.

Urged by a friend to make his own films, Tykwer began entering film festivals. He made and entered a short film titled, *Because,* about arguments he had been having with his girlfriend. He was encouraged to create by a fellow film maker, Rosa von Praunheim, whom he became close friends with. Tykwer credits her for much of his early success. She particularly inspired him to make films from his own experiences rather than focusing on fantasy and fiction. From as early as 1990, his films started to get critical acclaim and he was encouraged to continue to make short films. While these short films cost him a lot of money, he gained excellent experience and skill in film making.

Twyker began to work on feature length films, starting with a film called *Deadly Maria* which was released in Germany. It did not receive much attention but he continued with his dream of making films. Twyker founded a production company called "X Filme Creative Pool" with three fellow film makers Stefan Arndt, Wolfgang Becker and Dani Levy. Twyker and Becker worked

© Five Senses Education Pty Ltd

together on screen plays while Twyker was producing his second feature film called *Wintersleepers*. This second film gained Twyker the attention of German critics and did very well in the film festival circuits. These endeavours were costing Twyker a lot of money so he needed to quickly produce another film that would bring in some funds for the company. In 1998 the resulting film, *Run Lola Run* was made and it became an international success, making seven million in the United States alone when released in 1999.

Twyker has continued to make films both in German and English. One film released in 2002 called *Heaven* starred the Australian actress Cate Blanchett. In 2006 he made a short film called *True* for a film festival in Paris which starred the famous American actress, Natalie Portman. He collaborated with a highly experienced producer called Bernd Eichinger on an adaptation of a book by Patrick Süskind titled, *Perfume*. In 2012 he produced *Cloud Atlas*.

# PLOT OUTLINE

Telephone Conversation between Lola and Manni

Opening credits

Lola explains to Manni what has happened to her bike

Manni explains to Lola how he got the diamonds and how he lost the money

Lola begins running. She narrowly misses the lady with the pram. A flashforward of her life is shown

Lola narrowly misses a group of nuns

Lola narrowly misses being hit by a car but that car hits another white car.

Lola interacts with a boy on a bike. His future is shown in a small sequence.

Lola catches her father with another woman.

Lola passes a woman in the hallway and her future is shown.

Lola saves Manni from being arrested and together they rob the store.

Lola's father unsympathetically throws her out of his office.

Lola and Manni's relationship is explored in the "red scene".

Lola is shot by a police officer accidentally.

© Five Senses Education Pty Ltd

Lola is tripped by the boy with the dog as she runs down the stairs. This slows her down.

Lola's second run begins. She runs into the lady with the pram whose life changes after winning the lottery.

Lola narrowly runs over the car which crashed into the white car.

Lola catches her father in an argument about his affair. She unleashes her anger and is destructive, hurling objects in his office.

Lola holds her father hostage and robs the bank. She escapes due to incompetent police officers.

Lola runs into the homeless guy with Manni's money.

Lola distracts the ambulance driver who hits the pane of glass.

Lola makes it to Manni who hears her calling. However he gets hit by the ambulance.

Manni and Lola have a red scene where they discuss how Lola would feel if Manni died.

Lola runs again but this time the guy with the bike sells it to the homeless man with Manni's money.

Lola misses catching her father and instead wins all the money at a casino after riding with the ambulance.

Manni catches the homeless guy with his money and returns it to the men who are after their money.

Manni and Lola walk away alive, healthy and with one hundred thousand German marks!

# PLOT SUMMARY WITH COMMENTARY

## The Opening Sequence

The film opens with two quotes. One is from a poet, T.S Eliot. He wrote in the 'Four Quartets', "We shall not cease from exploration, and the end of all our exploring will be to arrive where we started and know the place for the first time". Read more at http://www.brainyquote.com/quotes/quotes/t/tseliot109032.html#udIH4iptAA5PU9de.99. Many have grappled with the meaning of this quote which is linked to our journey through life. The second quote is from a German soccer coach called S. Herberger. He led Germany to win the World Cup in 1954. Consequently, he is very important to the people of Germany. The quote is roughly translated to, "After the game is before the game". If you listen to the director's commentary, the actress playing Lola comments that people usually laugh when they see this quote. This is most likely because this is a serious film with deep and insightful commentary on life and being human.

The first quote seems appropriate as it is from a serious, highly acclaimed poet. The second seems to be less serious as it is by a soccer coach. It, however, reflects the Germans' and the director's love of soccer. To them, it is one of the most important aspects of life. A quote from a soccer coach is seen to have the same level of importance to the Germans as one of the world's most noted poets. This makes people laugh whilst also embedding the film in a German context.

As the credits appear, a talisman is swaying back and forth over the screen like the pendulum of a grandfather clock. This symbolises time, a significant theme in the film. Also, the talisman appears

© Five Senses Education Pty Ltd

to be from ancient times and depicts an aggressive looking face. This sets the atmosphere for a dramatic story, which has, through use of suspense and other elements, aspects of a horror or a thriller. The talisman is emphasised as it is lit from the front, reflecting a bright orange colour that stands out on the plain black background. It is also emphasised when it stops moving and the camera pans in for a close up. The camera then pans to show a clock, a low angle shot. As always, the low angle shot emphasises the significance of the clock and puts the audience in a submissive position in relation to the clock, or what it symbolises,time.

Therefore, immediately, the audience recognises that time is being depicted as highly important and possibly as having more control over life than humans do. It is seen as a central theme in the film. Again, this is emphasised as the creature on the clock opens its mouth and appears to be swallowing the audience. The ticking sound effects emphasise the notion of time. Additionally, the fast paced music reflects the constant movement of Lola.

After the audience has been swallowed by the creature, the scene changes to images of people who are out of focus and rushing around. The beat of the music quickens to emphasise the speed of the people. Almost everyone is wearing black and looks similar. Their faces are not visible, making them anonymous. This technique indicates that the people in this scene are not very important. It is their movements that we should be focusing on. These people could be anyone. Even the viewer.

There is no scene as such, simply a bright white colour in the background, emphasising that setting is not important. Most people have their heads down and are not drawing attention to themselves. Indiscernible whispering sounds can be heard. As the camera pans through these people, the audience feels as if they too are struggling through a crowd and are anonymous. This sets a face-paced atmosphere that is tense and almost claustrophobic. Cast members stand out due to their colourful dress, upright stance and demanding gaze. We will find as the film progresses that Lola and Manni are also depicted in the film as being fairly anonymous. No one in the street recognises them or knows about the intense drama that is unfolding in their lives.

Time is used as a technique in the opening scene. The film is sped up to emphasise the speed with which people are moving. It is also slowed down to focus in on certain individuals. This emphasises certain characters that the composer wants the audience to be aware of. These characters, as mentioned, are looking directly at the camera, standing still and wearing something bright to emphasise that they are not meant to be anonymous to the audience. These people are, however, still anonymous to the other characters in the scene who continue to walk past them. Again soccer is emphasised by the police officer kicking the ball and the camera panning to follow the movement of the ball. This panning brings the shot to a long shot where the audience sees a pattern emerging amongst the people. They spell out the name Lola Rennt which is the title of the film in German.

Again, the camera work is quick and unpredictable, reflecting the action that will be taking place in the film. The camera pans in to a close up shot of the "o" in Lola and goes through the letter where we are met with a new scene. This is the first of the animation scenes that are edited into the live action of the film. The animation is in dull colours, primarily blue and black. A long road stretches out before Lola and she is running quickly along it avoiding real obstacles such as bats and imagined obstacles such

   © Five Senses Education Pty Ltd

as vicious creatures. Due to the dull, dreary palate of colours used, Lola is salient due to her bright, red hair. She grabs at objects such as spider webs which make breaking noises when they collapse. This contributes to a chaotic atmosphere.

Finally Lola runs through a tunnel with teeth all around her, symbolising the danger she will face on this journey. She is running towards a clock at the end of this tunnel, again emphasising the significance of time in this film. Lola is finally sucked into the animation of blue, swirling with wide eyes and messy hair. This represents her own feelings of losing control of time and her own life which will become evident in the film. The music continues to be fast paced with strained noise emphasising the stressful situation.

The next scene introduces the characters and corresponding actors. The actors and characters are presented to the audience in a manner reminiscent of a police mug shot. We see an image of them in profile, from the back and then finally from the front. Each movement is edited to emphasise that it is a separate shot. The sound of a camera clicks in between each of the shots. This creates an atmosphere of fragmentation which is a technique throughout the film. The images are also edited with a scratched surface put over the top of the screen. You will notice bits of scratches and what appears to be small fragments of dirt over the shot. This unpolished look highlights the chaotic atmosphere and portrays an unfinished or rushed look to the film.

The actors' names also appear as a door closing on the actor and are accompanied by the sound of heavy metal slamming. This reminds the audience of a gaol cell door slamming. The police and gaol images establish a crime genre. This highlights the drama and seriousness of the film. Manni, a protagonist, faces serious consequences if he does not get the money, the one hundred thousand marks he needs.

The next scene is an extreme overhead shot of a city. This again portrays a sense of anonymity. Everyone is getting on with their life and the city is still buzzing and functioning while the two people we are about to meet will have their lives changed forever. The camera pans from this extreme overhead shot into an apartment, through a window into Lola's room, taking the audience on a fast paced ride. By this time, the audience should be very much in touch with the chaotic, fast paced nature of the film. (Additional resource - http://www.artofthetitle.com/title/run-lola-run/)

**The Telephone Conversation with flashbacks.**

A close up shot of the bright red telephone is seen. The phone is ringing loudly. The bright red colour stands out, as does Lola's bright red hair. She has clearly been expecting this phone call and answers it with a distressed look on her face and an anxious tone in her voice.

The scene that follows uses editing as a technique to emphasise the chaos that is unfolding. The scenes jump between Lola in her bedroom and Manni, also looking distressed, in a bright yellow phone booth. The first time we see Manni he has his back towards us but then the camera pans into the booth and captures an extreme close up of Manni's distressed face. These camera techniques continue to emphasise the fragmented and chaotic nature of the events that are occurring. Rapid editing and alternating low angle, long shots, then close up camera shots

© Five Senses Education Pty Ltd

heighten the feeling of fragmented time. One of the long shots of Lola reveals the room she is in. It has a dull colour palette and is a messy, unordered room. This symbolises Lola's unordered and complicated lifestyle. The colour palette is dull with mismatched colours and furniture reflecting the haphazard nature of her life. The conversation between them is very heated as they argue about what Manni is going to do. Manni is clearly anxious and shouting. He is panicked and is desperate to try and resolve his situation of having to get money quickly.

The scene uses a flashback, again capturing the fragmented style that is developing. To emphasise this, the section has been filmed in black and white, possibly to suggest it is in the past, although it is evidently in the recent past. Lola is buying what appears to be cigarettes when her moped (bike) is stolen by someone outside the store. She chases after them, with the timing of the event again being sped up by the director and slowed down when it is clear that Lola will not catch the thief. This emphasises her helplessness.

We then return to the telephone conversation when Manni realises what has happened. He was relying on Lola to be at the place to pick him up but, as her bike was stolen, he had to catch the train. Lola and Manni's past continues to be shown in black and white images. The audience becomes aware of the paths that have led these two people to their current dramatic situation. It appears that Manni has bought diamonds from some mob-like characters. He delivers the diamonds to an elderly gentleman who indicates that they are diamonds by the specialised eyepiece he is wearing while he inspects them. We then have an overhead shot of a lot of money being placed in a bag which Manni is carrying.

Again, this action is edited with colour film which shows Manni and Lola continuing their conversation. As they explain what is happening, black and white images of past events appear. Manni is on the train when a homeless man falls down. He helps the homeless man get up and we see a shot of two police officers staring into the camera with a knowing look on their faces. Manni quickly but casually exits the train, a habit he has picked up by being constantly in trouble with the police, and realises once off the train that he has left the money where he was sitting.

Editing is used to show Manni's thoughts as he is walking off the train. As he is realising that he has left the money, an image of the bag of money sitting alone on the train is shown to the audience. The image shapes Manni's thoughts. His facial expressions register realisation and shock. The music emphasises Manni's desperation to get back to the money as it has stretched, pained sounds and a quickened pace. The officers grab him and he struggles to get free of them.

Several shots follow which tell the story of what will happen to the money. We see a shot of the homeless man staring directly into the camera as the train doors close. This tells the audience that he is very aware of the situation and has been watching Manni struggle to get back on the train. We then see a close up shot of the bag of money resting on the seat. The fact that the homeless man continues to look into the camera, and therefore at Manni, in a calm manner, simply standing, suggests that he is going to take the money.

Manni's reaction to the abandoned bag has indicated to the homeless man that there is something precious inside it. The camera shows a close up of the homeless man in colour. Perhaps

© Five Senses Education Pty Ltd

this indicates that this is the latest incident in a chain of events, and he is gloriously aware of his finding.

Manni and Lola continue their conversation in current time with Manni's continuing story being depicted in images. We also see in bright colour and rapid editing the thoughts of Manni and what the homeless man might do with the money. Manni's ideas of all the countries he will visit are depicted in glamorous, idyllic, colour images.

The last of this sequence of images is a black and white image of a man. The quick editing and fast paced images which are displayed to the quick beat of the music emphasise again the concept of time and a lack of control. The flashbacks continue to depict Manni's story as he is pressured by the thugs who want their money for the diamonds. The shots of the violence towards Manni are taken on an angle symbolising dysfunction.

We return to the telephone conversation one last time with the music continuing to reflect the fast pace of action. Manni is clearly desperate and is yelling in an aggressive way at Lola, emphasising his distress and concern that she cannot help him. Lola, up to this point, seems to be simply distressed as she takes all of this information in and tried to reassure Manni that things will be okay. However, she reaches a point where she must release the tension that she, and the audience, are feeling. She does this with a loud, high pitched scream. The high pitch smashes some bottles in her room, emphasising the release that occurs within her and her call to action.

After this, there are some shots around her room. They show the ripped and dishevelled blinds, a single Polaroid of herself and Manni in an embrace indicating their intimate relationship, some dolls haphazardly lined up in her room, some clothed, some not and a turtle moving slowly across the room, presumably as a result of the scream. These shots slow down the pace of the film momentarily and emphasise the scream that has occurred. It also allows us to see the details of Lola's room and her relationship with Manni. This introduces a small intermission in the tension, yet it resumes again almost immediately as the telephone conversation continues.

The composer indicates Manni's plan. We have long shots focussing on the supermarket across the street from where Manni is standing in his telephone booth. The shots of the conversation vary between close up and mid shots of the characters so the facial expressions and distress are emphasised. Close up shots also emphasise the drama of the situation.

The town clock is shown often throughout the film to emphasise the role time plays. Also, Manni's telephone card running out indicates how time, or the lack of it, is often the thing in this film that makes the characters take action. A close up of the television in Lola's room shows an image of dominoes falling. This symbolises time running out as each domino falls. This idea is emphasised by Lola's slow, calculated turn towards the camera, emphasising she has decided to take action. Again, an image of Lola's clock, panning and then close up shots of her staring at it reflects the theme of time. Lola throws the phone receiver in the air and the camera follows it as it flies across the room. This occurs in slow motion and builds suspense in the film. The sequence finishes with many shots of Lola edited into small, fragmented segments.

© Five Senses Education Pty Ltd

She is thinking about what she is going to do, as indicated by her hands massaging her temples. She sometimes appears dishevelled and the fast pace of the editing shows she is feeling pressured. Time is further distorted in this sequence. After we see shots of Lola, the receiver lands precisely on the phone cradle. We realise that time does not run chronologically in this film and we must pay attention to the detail to understand what is happening.

The next scene is introduced by an animated character pulling the next shot over the previous one. He is dressed formally in a suit and bow tie. He later appears in the film as a real person. The scene he introduces shows Lola standing in the room with the camera spinning around her in a close up shot. This emphasises the chaos building within her.

The audience is surprised by the people she considers, which includes children, as she is trying to get one hundred thousand Deutschmarks (marks). This was roughly equivalent to eighty thousand Australian dollars. She considers many people in her desperation. Most of the shots of the people are very rapid. One, however, lasts for longer. It indicates the person to whom she is going to appeal for money. She says aloud, "Papa" telling the audience that she is going to seek help from her father. She then leaves the shot, emphasising her exit by leaving an empty shot for the audience. Her father's eyes follow her, even though he is simply an image of her thoughts. He shakes his head. The audience is constantly given signs that Lola's journey to help Manni is not going to be easy.

## THE FIRST RUN

Lola runs out the door with the camera following. The camera takes a slight detour as it goes into a room on the right showing a long shot of a woman sitting on a couch talking on the telephone with an alcoholic drink in her hand. This is the only shot that stays the same in all of the sequences. As the camera circles around the female character, the audience can see an animated version of Lola running on the television. The camera pans towards the television and to a point where the camera is no longer in the room and the image is completely animated. The image shows Lola running down the stairs. The stairs, however, are drawn in a way to appear as if they are treacherous and endless. Lola appears to be disproportionate and is dwarfed by this never-ending staircase.

The animation shows an extreme close up of Lola's face as she runs towards the camera and down the stairs. This heightens the suspense as our first indication of what is in front of her comes from the shocked expression on her face. We see her run past the boy and his vicious dog. A close up of the dog's barred teeth indicates that this was a near miss for her. When Lola reaches for the door and opens it, the camera returns to live footage. The music the whole time is fast paced and saying, "I wish I was a ruler, then they'd understand". This further emphasises the fast pace of the action in the film but also Lola's feelings of helplessness and desperation as she runs to try and save Manni's life.

The shots of Lola running tend to be a mix of several different shots, again emphasising the fragmented nature and lack of order in the events that are occurring. The first are extreme long shots which show Lola both running towards the camera and

    © Five Senses Education Pty Ltd

running away from the camera into the streets. While on her run, Lola encounters several obstacles which are important. These details change in the subsequent runs and therefore alter her life significantly. As she turns a corner, we see her narrowly miss a lady walking with a baby in a stroller. As Lola knocks her slightly, the camera shows a mid-shot of the woman abusing Lola. Lola continues to run. While she is running, the audience sees images of the people she has encountered.

Again, we see that they are not live footage as they are edited into single shots. They are clearly depicting still shots of people i.e. photographs. However, the photographs are candid which allows the audience to see the truth behind these people's lives rather than staged photos you might put up in your living room. The photos of the woman and the child in the pram show her future. The sequence depicts a troubled relationship and that she will lose her child as the police will take it away, presumably as a result of some form of neglect. It shows her distress which results in her stealing someone else's baby from its pram.

The shots of Lola running under the bridge again incorporate varying speeds, camera shots and angles. Slow motion is used to emphasise the strained expression on Lola's face and therefore to suggest the speed and length of time she has been running. Front on, close up shots are also combined with profile, long angle shots of Lola running to keep the audience interested whilst also indicating that she was running for a long time. The editing of these demand and offer shots is not always cut and then they morph straight into the next shot. Occasionally the shots are blended together as one fades in, the other fades out to show the passage of time.

The next sequence of shots show Lola's father in his office with a woman crying. They are intimate and she is asking him if he wants to have a child with her. This is the first time in the film that we see two people having a discussion with one another in a calm, stable environment.

This serves to emphasise the situation that Lola walks into and how she must try and adapt to the situation after her experiences so far. When the camera shows a long shot of the room we realise that they too are experiencing their own crisis. Theirs, however, is more conservative, possibly reflective of their age. Lola's father is sitting on the floor which is unusual for an office and they are having a conversation yet the woman is not facing him.

Lola continues to face obstacles in her path such as a group of nuns walking and taking up much of the path. In this instance Lola runs through the middle of the two lines of nuns. We also see a male character with a red shirt on a bicycle who speaks to Lola. We get a flash forward sequence showing him being pushed off his bike, mugged and, as a consequence, meeting the woman of his dreams in the hospital. He dates and eventually marries her. This shows how one incident in someone's life, however minor, can lead to a significant moment.

Lola continues to run through a construction site and is approaching her father's office. As she approaches a car is exiting a tunnel onto the street and cannot see Lola approaching on the footpath. The car narrowly misses Lola. The driver, as a result of watching Lola run by, crashes into a white car. The people in the white car are the thugs who are after Manni. The man in the car is named Mr Myer and is actually on his way to pick up Lola's father.

© Five Senses Education Pty Ltd

The next scene shows Manni getting out of the telephone booth and attempting to return the telephone card to the blind woman. She does not accept the card but continues walking. Again, a shot of the clock is shown so the audience can keep track of the timing of the film. Manni is waiting until 12pm, noon, to enter the store. Back with Lola, she turns a corner and runs straight past the homeless man who has Manni's money.

The next scene clearly shows the affair between Lola's father and the unknown woman. Lola enters her father's place of work, which happens to be a bank. She is clearly recognised by the security man and is allowed upstairs. As Lola runs along a corridor we recognise the woman from the opening scenes walking along the corridor towards Lola. She has to turn to get out of Lola's way. The flash-forward of her life is quite traumatic. She has a car accident and becomes permanently injured. She appears to take her own life in a very bloody manner and is buried in a cemetery.

When Lola enters her father's office she catches them in an intimate moment. She is clearly shocked as her father's mistress introduces herself and then leaves. The following conversation between Lola and her father clearly indicates that he does not know her very well. He is unaware that she has a boyfriend. He seems quite uncaring to his daughter's situation and again Lola screams in frustration. She smashes the glass clock on the wall, indicating that time is fragmented and chaotic but also that she is losing control of it. Her father is clearly embarrassed by Lola's disturbance and ushers her quickly from the building. He is annoyed at security for allowing her access and Lola leaves the building feeling dejected.

After Lola has been kicked out of the bank, there is a slow motion shot of her turning to face the camera. You can see a young woman in the background walking towards Lola. However, when the woman gets to Lola she is an old lady, emphasising how the directors are playing with time in the editing process. The music starts again with a low, quick beat indicating that she is going to run again. Lola asks the old woman what time it is and she discovers she has almost no time left to get to Manni. She starts running again.

An overhead shot shows Lola running through a piazza, or an open space. Again this is an extremely high angle, overhead shot showing the insignificance of Lola as she runs to perhaps the most significant moment in her life. Manni is still in the phone booth checking the time and waiting until he enters the supermarket. Lola is seen running alongside a red van, an ambulance. As the van is being driven, men in yellow overalls carry a pane of glass. The driver has to stop so he doesn't hit the pane. This slows Lola down and she too has to stop momentarily.

A shot of Manni walking towards the bank shows his wallet in close up in his back pocket, and the supermarket in long shot in the background. A low angle shot of the clock indicates that time is up and Manni enters the supermarket in the next shot. The ambulance that Lola just had to stop for drives past in the background indicating to the audience that Lola is not far away. The screen then splits into two shots; one showing Lola and the other showing Manni. This split screen technique then continues to show Lola, Manni and the clock. This symbolises 'time' as really almost being a third character in the film. At one point we see Lola in the background at the end of the street in Manni's shot and Manni in the background in Lola's shot, indicating just how

© Five Senses Education Pty Ltd

close she was to getting there in time. Lola calls out to Manni but he doesn't hear her. He enters the supermarket and proceeds with the robbery.

## The Supermarket Robbery

The editing of the shots in this sequence is significant. The time of each of the shots gets shorter and shorter. The scene has been filmed several times and several of the same shots have been used again and again so that Manni says the same lines several times. The editing time between shots gets shorter and shorter as the tension rises. This shows again how time has been manipulated to express the confusion and chaos that is felt by everyone involved in the event.

Lola arrives and Manni and Lola have an uncharacteristically calm conversation. It is almost dream like. They speak slowly and calmly to each other again, manipulating time. Lola assists Manni in the robbery and there are several shots of her that gradually become closer and closer.

They both manage to escape and there are shots of them running in slow motion. The music is a very slow, old fashioned tune with lyrics such as, "What a difference a day makes," reflecting the major themes of the film. The music seems to contradict the action of the film as it is an old, slow crooning type song and yet this is undoubtedly the climax of the film with a lot of action. However, the lyrics are highly appropriate.

## The Shooting Sequence

As Lola and Manni are trapped by the police, the camera circles around them emphasising the chaotic feelings they must be experiencing. As Manni throws the bag of money, the police officer watches it and shoots Lola in the chest.

The next scene is shot with a red film over the top so everything in the scene appears to be red. Manni and Lola are having an intimate moment discussing their relationship. The close up shots emphasise intimacy and the private nature of their conversation. The red lighting reflects the inherent passion of the situation.

This scene is very important in revealing the passion and love between Lola and Manni. This scene helps the audience to get to know the characters and to understand why Lola would run the way she does to get to Manni and try and help him. The passion and intimacy in this scene explains the drama and the desperation of the characters in the action sequences.

The action returns to Lola lying on the ground with a close up, overhead shot of her face. The previous scene sets the audience up to feel moved as Lola appears to be dying. Without the previous scene, the audience may not know Lola and Manni and their relationship well enough to be moved by her shooting and Manni's consequent heartbreak.

This scene is edited with scenes of the red bag containing the money, flying up in the air. Again it is out of time as, by the time Lola has been shot, the bag would have already hit the ground. We also have flash back scenes edited in to show the telephone receiver flying through the air in much the same manner as the bag. We get close up shots of both the bag and the receiver very

© Five Senses Education Pty Ltd

quickly edited together and showing Lola's face as she remains on the ground after her shooting. These scenes emphasise the events that have happened previously and the role of chance in this film as the phone receiver and the bag of money seem to reflect the unpredictable or "up in the air" nature of Lola's life at this point in time.

# PLOT ACTIVITIES FOR THE FIRST RUN

1. Plot the significant events that led to the demise of Lola in this run. The significant events will include the people she met and the moments that were both sped up and slowed down.

2. Why do you think the director has introduced the lives of other characters along the way? What message is being strengthened by including flash forwards?

3. Reflect on Lola's actions throughout her run. Did she do anything that could suggest she deserved her final plight or is there no logical cause and effect here?

4. Twyker has used various film techniques to identify symbols and other themes of the narrative for the reader. Identify three themes of the text and explain the effectiveness of Twyker's film techniques in portraying these to the audience.

5. This is the only run in which the audience witnesses Lola's moped being stolen and the reason that Manni had any money in the first place. Why do you think the director has included this in this run yet chose to omit this in the next runs?

6. The opening credits highlight people we will meet in the film. What techniques does the director use to highlight significant people before we even meet them? Why does he choose to highlight these anonymous individuals as significant characters?

7. Use the analysis of the opening credits to start practising extended writing about techniques. Write a paragraph describing the effectiveness of techniques in introducing and emphasising the theme of time for the audience.

© Five Senses Education Pty Ltd

# THE SECOND RUN

The second run starts from when the phone receiver is hung up by Lola. She runs out of her room and again past the room with the woman on the chair, drinking alcohol. This scene does not change and Lola does not interact with this woman in any way. Again, animation is seen as Lola runs down the stairs. This animation, however, is much shorter than the first. Also, when Lola runs down the stairs the boy with his dog at the bottom, trips Lola over. This inevitably slows her down. The close up shots of Lola's animated face show her distress and the chaos that ensues. When she arrives at the bottom of the stairs, live footage is used again and the actress playing Lola appears to have fallen down the stairs and landed at the bottom. The close up shots of her face emphasise her distress. This is also the first instance when we see Lola's original journey being interrupted and consequently altered by someone else. Lola initially appears to struggle but is soon running again.

As Lola turns the corner, she runs more directly into the woman with the pram. The woman turns around and abuses Lola but then we get a flash-forward in her life and realise that everything has changed for her. No longer does she lose her child but she wins lotto. The images depict a happy family who have clearly changed their lifestyle as a result of their big win. Again, this is showing how one small aspect of someone's life can change his or her life significantly. In this case, we don't know exactly what changes but it could be that she puts in the lotto ticket or that she simply wins the lottery.

We see different images of Lola running the second time around but they are still often the overhead, extreme long shots which show Lola as an anonymous person running through a busy city setting. Lola runs through the group of nuns but this time, she is distracted by one of them wearing sunglasses. She slows down momentarily but then continues to have her conversation with the boy in the red shirt on the bicycle. The boy on the bike no longer gets mugged and no longer ends up in hospital meeting the woman he is going to marry. Instead, we do not see any mugging, rather that the man ends up becoming homeless and possibly a drug addict.

Lola is behind time in terms of where she was in the first sequence as a result of all the obstacles she has encountered. The car still runs into the white vehicle, just towards the back rather than towards the front. Therefore, we can conclude she is only a couple of seconds behind.

Lola actually runs directly into the homeless man carrying Manni's money. She runs into him, however, further down the street rather than when she gets around the corner. This still slows her down.

## The Bank Robbery

Lola runs into the bank and passes the woman who was seen previously. This time the woman's face does not even appear and she is simply another person Lola passes. Previously she was involved in an accident and committed suicide.

When Lola enters her father's office he is in a heated exchange with his lover rather than the intimate embrace she first encountered. The woman in the previous scene asked Lola's father if he wanted to have a child with her, to which he responded positively. Lola

© Five Senses Education Pty Ltd

walks in, to an atmosphere that clearly indicates they are having an affair. However, we realise that she would have continued to tell him that the child may not be his. This results in the argument Lola walks in on the second time.

Other staff members are listening outside the door. Yelling is occurring as Lola's father is distressed about the news he is hearing. We discover more about Lola's life as she, and consequently we, become privy to the conversation. It appears that Lola's mother is an alcoholic and Lola is one of three siblings. Her father still feels some sense of duty towards them but is clearly resentful of the fact.

Lola becomes very distressed when it appears that her father will not help her, despite the fact that she has just found that her father is having an affair with someone else. Lola's father has an abrupt manner. He is willing to give her money just so she will leave him alone. Lola is also berated by his mistress who accuses Lola of being rude for barging in on her private conversation. This altercation allows the composers to ensure that the audience feels sorry for Lola and cares about what happens to her in her life.

This time Lola's father slaps her across the face and Lola consequently destroys his office before leaving. She ends up leaving but feeling more desperate than when she arrived. However, in the previous version, Lola's father calmly ushers her out of the building. This time Lola screams, " What?" at the woman who was previously anonymous and runs, crying. The police officer says to Lola that today doesn't seem to be her lucky day, again suggesting that each day can alter your life and luck. Lola takes his gun and returns to her father's office. The low angle shots of her striding back towards her father's office show her in a position of power. She is determined to save Manni.

In the first version Lola does not know how to use the gun but Manni helps her. She almost kills an elderly security officer. It seems as if she transfers this newly acquired gun knowledge into her second version of events as she knows how to aim and shoot. Whereas previously it was her father leading Lola out of the bank, this time it is Lola who escorts her father out of the bank. On her way out, the previously anonymous woman in the stairway tries to confront Lola and her future changes. Her flash-forward now shows her meeting a man (the teller at the front) and falling in love. They are seemingly a very conservative couple, however, they privately participate in sordid sex games.

Lola points the gun at the man in the teller booth and makes him count out one hundred thousand marks. She makes him fetch the rest of the money from downstairs, despite the warnings from her father that the police will be there soon. Lola reminds him that he has told her they never make it in time anyway. Lola and her father sit in silence until the teller returns. He gives her the money in a garbage bag and she leaves. She drops the gun and runs outside to find the building surrounding by police. She looks around, clearly feeling dejected about being caught. She is waved away, however, as they clearly do not think that Lola is the bank robber. The police officers surround the building.

Eventually, one of the swat team remove Lola while they prepare to go into the bank and arrest the bank robber. This stroke of luck results in Lola running away with the money. She asks the elderly woman the time but doesn't wait for the answer.

© Five Senses Education Pty Ltd

## The Ambulance Sequence

In this version, Lola asks the ambulance driver for a lift so she can get to Manni faster. As the driver is distracted by Lola, he fails to see the men carrying the pane of glass and consequently drives straight through it. Lola continues to run with the repetition of the split screen technique showing Lola and Manni and the clock. This time when Lola calls out to Manni he hears her and turns around. They run to each other in what appears to be a romantic moment for them both. Manni then gets hit by the ambulance which, in the first version, went straight past him. Manni was hit right before Lola's eyes.

At this point, everything occurs in slow motion. Lola drops the bag of money and finds Manni dying. This time it is his dying thoughts, which lead us to the red scene. Lola is smoking and talking about how she would never forget Manni if he died. This moment shows how Lola feels about Manni.

# PLOT ACTIVITIES FOR THE SECOND RUN

1.  In this run, it is Manni who loses his life at the end. Reflect on the events that have occurred in this run. Is there any obvious cause and effect which may explain why Manni loses his life?

2.  Consider Lola's father. Outline what happens in the first run and then outline what Lola witnesses in the second run. How does this event significantly change the course of events for Lola?

3.  It becomes apparent that Lola has, in fact, learnt lessons from the first run she undertook, even though the runs seem to occur concurrently. What has Lola learnt and how does it help her in the next run?

4.  Lola's world, as represented through her costume and the bedroom setting, is vastly different from the world of her father, represented in his costume and banking world. Compare the two settings and evaluate how they reflect the values of the individual. Discuss the techniques used by the director to highlight the settings.

5.  Make a table with the first, second and third run labelled down the side and the individuals that provide flash forwards on the top. See over for an example. Fill in this table identifying the different experiences of the people and consider why their lives may have changed. Did they learnt from the past too?

© Five Senses Education Pty Ltd

|  | The man with the dog on the stairs | The lady with the pram, around the corner near Lola's apartment | The man on the bike after Lola runs through the group of nuns | The lady in Lola's father's office hallway |
|---|---|---|---|---|
| First Run |  |  |  |  |
| Second Run |  |  |  |  |
| Third Run |  |  |  |  |
| Identify any connections between the fate of these people and their actions. |  |  |  |  |

# THE THIRD RUN

The third run opens like the others with the woman talking on the phone. Her television depicts the animated version of Lola but this time she leaps over the dog and past the boy who previously tripped her over.

Lola runs past the lady with the pram and does not get abused by her. Her future has changed once again to reveal someone who goes on a spiritual journey and finds God.

This time the nuns do not move out of the way for Lola so she runs into the street to avoid hitting them. As she is not watching where she is going she runs into the boy on the bike and nearly knocks him off. This time the camera follows the guy on the bike rather than Lola. He goes into a fast food shop where the audience recognises the other customer as being the homeless guys with Manni's money. The boy on the bike realises that the homeless man has come in to quite a bit of money. He offers his bike for purchase.

Lola jumps onto the hood of the car this time to avoid being hit by it. The white car drives past and does not get hit this time as Lola is lying on the bonnet of the car preventing the man from driving it. Lola and the driver recognise each other but she continues running. Lola does not run into the homeless man as he is now on a bike.

## Lola's Father's Office

Lola's father is having an intense discussion with his mistress and is interrupted by Mr Myer's requests about when he is coming

© Five Senses Education Pty Ltd

down. Mr Meyer is the man in the car Lola keeps running into. He has recently avoiding running into the white car.

This time the split screen technique is used to indicate the race between Lola and her father as Lola attempts to catch him before he leaves the bank. This time Lola calls out to her father but he cannot hear her. Mr Meyer is telling Lola's father in the car that he has just had a "strange encounter" with Lola. Lola stops outside the bank and is inappropriately propositioned by the security guard.

Manni leaves the telephone booth and attempts to return the telephone card to the elderly blind woman waiting outside. As the woman asks Manni to wait, he is standing long enough to notice the homeless man cycle by with the bag of money sitting in the front basket of the bicycle. Manni chases after him and narrowly avoids being hit by another car. This time, it is the car that Mr Meyer and Lola's father are in. Mr Meyer still hits the white car though, almost as if this was always going to happen no matter what the circumstances surrounding the event. A motorbike rider was also involved in the accident and appears to have died. The audience wonders if this one fatality will allow Manni and/or Lola to live.

An extreme close up of Lola's profile reflects her thoughts as she begs someone to help her. She narrowly avoids being hit by a truck which she runs in front of. Lola sees this as a sign as she has been stopped right out the front of a casino. The lady at the counter gives her a break and allows her into the casino even though she is not properly dressed. Again, the theme of fate and chance is evident as Lola places her bets in the casino. She wins her first bet and makes a second bet so she can make up the rest of the money. She must risk everything in order to make the money she needs. Again, an official is generous in allowing her to have one more game, despite the fact she is not dressed appropriately. Once again Lola screams to let out her angst. She smashes glasses in the casino. Lola wins the money she needed in order to save Manni and chance is on her side this time. There is an effective long shot as Lola is leaving the casino, showing the staff and other patrons staring at her as she asks the teller to put her money in a bag. The music is primitive and raw, emphasising the fact that what has happened has been left up to fate and is out of the hands of mere mortals. Something quite dramatic and unpredictable occurred and everyone was in awe. A close up of the clock on the wall emphasises the theme of time and the fact that Lola's journey is far from over.

Manni has to pull a gun at the homeless man on the bike in order to get his money back. The homeless man recognises that it is Manni's money and allows him to take it. Manni apologises, recognising that this man has now also lost the money he found. Manni reluctantly accepts his request for the gun, clearly concerned that the man will immediately turn the gun on him and demand the money back. However, Manni gets away with the money.

Lola runs alongside the ambulance which again narrowly misses the pane of glass in the middle of the road. She jumps into the back of the ambulance and finds that the ambulance officers are working on a man who has been injured. She states that she belongs to him. They are clearly surprised by her ability to renew the man's health when they were trying to resuscitate him only a second ago. The ambulance officer is in awe of her power.

© Five Senses Education Pty Ltd

## The Casino

Lola is released from the ambulance in the middle of the intersection where the supermarket is located. She calls out and continues to look around. She finds Manni getting out of a black car, presumably the car belonging to the men he owes the money to. He is in a happy exchange with them. He walks towards her and asks if she has been running. The audience laughs as we realise that this is all Lola has been doing for the whole film.

He also asks her what she has in the bag and the audience realises that Lola still has all the money she has won. Not only have they settled Manni's debts but they are also now one thousand marks richer. This is, of course, the best possible scenario of them all and we are happy that this film has such a fairy tale ending for these protagonists.

# PLOT ACTIVITIES FOR THE THIRD RUN

1.  Why do you think this run works out for Lola? What has changed or what has she learnt that may have resulted in a success this time.

2.  Lola's other runs have all ended in tragedy where as in this run she saves two lives; one is the man in the ambulance and the other is Manni. She also walks away with a bag full of money. Why do you think the director has chosen to end this on such a positive note?

3.  Do you think that Lola and Manni deserve this level of success after their involvement in this crime? What message is being sent about involvement in criminal activity in this film?

4.  A Casino is a setting which revolves around the themes of luck and chance. How does the director use film techniques as well as setting to emphasise this theme?

5.  What fate befell the homeless man who took the money from the train? Trace his journey through these separate runs and discuss the message told through his life.

6.  What is the significance of the glass pane, the times it smashes and the times it is narrowly missed?

© Five Senses Education Pty Ltd

# GENERAL QUESTIONS ON PLOT

1. Discuss the irony seen when contrasting relationships. Support your answer with close textual referencing. Lola and Manni seem to have a solid, trusting and devoted relationship even though this is being expressed through the events of stolen money. Lola's wealthy father and career woman mistress are reflecting a stereotype of being highly moral and excellent members of society, yet are having a sordid affair.

2. Each run seems to replace the other in time. That is, the runs are all different but all happen at the same time. There is a clear introduction but no clear conclusion, simply the subsequent three runs. Which run do you think is the one that actually happened and why? There is no suggestion that this text is chronological so do not state that you think it is the last run.

3. As previously mentioned, there is no suggestion that these runs are chronological. Why do you think the director and screen writers have chosen to order these runs in this way? Do you think they are trying to promote a happy ending?

4. The final run shows a happy ending. What events in that final run suggest that chance has a larger part to play in our lives than the cause and effect of our actions? Make sure you discuss the techniques used by the director to suggest this.

5. In what ways can you identify with the themes and characters in this text? Where can you see the messages of the film in your own life?

# SETTING

## Lola's Room

The design of Lola's small room reflects what is happening in her life during the time of the film. It is a small room which has been decorated using a dull colour palette, including deep purples and browns. This could reflect the state of Lola's life in terms of feeling depressed about what has been happening. It is, however, more likely a design choice on the part of the composers so they are not drawing attention to the room, but rather to Lola and her current predicament. If there were bright, shiny things in the room, the audience may be distracted by these things, rather than focusing on the intense emotional and dramatic situation between Lola and Manni.

Lola's room appears to be very messy and disordered. This reflects Lola's life. When she asks her father for money he tells her to get a job, indicating that Lola is unemployed and has probably been unemployed for quite some time, otherwise this comment would not have been made so quickly. She also has broken blinds, empty beer bottles, half dressed dolls and other items around the house. The only decorative item she has is a Polaroid of herself and Manni that has been stuck to the wall. This indicates that Lola's dwelling is either only temporary or that she has simply neglected to fix her surroundings. This suggests that Lola has perhaps also been neglecting to look after herself. The fact that she is in love with someone who is supplying what one can only assume are stolen diamonds also suggests that she is not making the best choices for herself in her life.

© Five Senses Education Pty Ltd

One last point worth mentioning is the lighting in Lola's room. Her room is not very well lit, emphasising the dull colours but also the idea that this room is neglected and perhaps even that Lola does not spend a lot of time there.

Consequently, techniques such as colour palette, design and editing (we are only shown dishevelled details of Lola's room such as empty bottles and broken blinds) emphasise the chaotic nature of Lola's life at the moment.

## The Telephone Booth

As with Lola's room, the telephone booth is one of the brightest things on the street. This makes sure the audience is not distracted by other things and focuses on Manni and his dilemma. Also, there are many close up shots which ensure that the audience is focused on him.

The phone booth is positioned on a cross roads which reflects where Manni is in his life at the moment. He must decide between robbing the supermarket and facing the thugs to whom he owes money. The shots of Manni in the phone booth show the supermarket, "Bolle" and a café called, "The Spiral Café" behind him. This café's title can be seen as symbolic as Manni's life is also spiralling out of control. At the time of their conversation, he only has twenty minutes to get the money to the people to whom he owes it.

The phone booth is very small and we, the audience, get the sense that Manni is almost hiding until it is time to leave. Once he leaves the booth, he must make a decision that will change his life and put him in danger, no matter what he chooses. The phone booth is covered in graffiti and also appears to be grimy, reflecting the situation that Manni has found himself in. It is not a glamorous image of crime, however, it seems a realistic one.

## The Streets

The streets represented in the film are the typical small lanes and back streets of Berlin which one can easily get lost in. Lola, however, knows her way around. We see her old, red brick apartment from the outside and it supports our already formed notion that Lola is struggling financially. Her home is certainly not palatial from the outside.

We often only see Lola in profile. We do not know where she is running to. This allows the director to manipulate the audience and adds to the suspense regarding Lola's destination. Lola literally bumps into people as she turns alley ways. She does not suspect there may be people around the corner such as the lady with the pram or the homeless man.

The streets represented are very dirty and many of the walls, such as the walls where the lady with the pram is walking, are graffitied. The setting supports the notion that Lola is living amidst crime and may be involved in crime. This is not an attractive neighbourhood. The woman yells slander at Lola even though Lola has simply bumped her. However as much as we are positioned to feel sorry for Lola and empathise with her, she has been involved in criminal activity.

There are a lot of unappealing, older style apartment buildings in the area, again supporting the idea that she is running through a

© Five Senses Education Pty Ltd

low socioeconomic area. The surroundings seem to be incomplete and fragmented with a lot of construction work going on.

Finally, the supermarket and the alley outside the supermarket where Lola and Manni are caught are similar to the street images. The fact that Lola and Manni become trapped in the alley way reflect the fact that they were always trapped and had to do something wrong, i.e. rob a supermarket, in order to escape. The only way that one of them was going to escape this time was through death which both Lola and Manni encounter. The lighting of these shots shows a grim perspective of Berlin which reflects the lives of Lola and Manni at this time. In the final scene, when they are walking away with the money, the lighting is brighter and suggests new hope for the couple.

## The Office

The street scenes are juxtaposed with Lola's father's office which has bright, white blinds. These, unlike Lola's, are clean and unbroken. The clean, utilitarian window coverings reflects Lola's father and his conservative, albeit hidden, nature. He appears one way but is actually another. He is, of course, concealing his affair and his highly styled office is concealing his true nature.

The bank foyer is very simple but glamorous with a large picture of a bank note above the elevator. This reflects both the priorities of the bank and Lola's father. He seems unemotional and more concerned about money than his daughter's welfare. The long hallway is narrow with fluorescent lighting. It could be seen as a metaphor for Lola as she is thinking that her father is the light at the end of the tunnel and the only one who can help her.

# CHARACTER ANALYSIS

There are two main characters in the film, Lola and Manni. The minor characters impact on the two central characters and affect their lives in some way. Make sure when you are discussing characters in essays, you are commenting on how they have been visually represented by the composer. Consider costuming, stance and body language.

## Lola

Lola is the main character in the film. The audience follows her journey. The film opens with Lola finding out her boyfriend, Manni has lost the money for a job they were doing. They must find one hundred thousand marks within twenty minutes or the thugs they were working with will pursue them and kill them. Manni believes it is Lola's fault as, when her moped was stolen, she was no longer able to pick up Manni after he had received the money. As a result he had to catch a train and he left the money on the train.

We see Lola's dishevelled, run down apartment as a reflection of where she has been heading in her life. She has no colour in her apartment and her hair seems to be her most vibrant aspect. Many people have speculated as to why Lola's hair is red. It could represent her passion and the energy which she shows as she tries to save Manni. It could also be seen as contrasting Lola with her environment to highlight she is different and has something to offer.

Lola's relationship with her father is seen in this film and the audience seems better informed about the affair between her

 © Five Senses Education Pty Ltd

father and her father's lover than Lola. The audience witnesses conversations about children and her pregnancy to another man. When Lola walks into his office, he focuses on how he can get her to leave. He is not pleased to see her. He is shocked she is involved in such a situation and was unaware she even had a boyfriend.

Lola and her father do not communicate very often or simply do not communicate well. Lola is surprised to see another woman in her father's life. Lola's father indicates that he cannot leave his family, particularly as his wife is sick. His lover, however, comments that Lola's mother is an alcoholic. We also discover that Lola is one of two siblings.

Two images of Lola's father are conveyed. One is the image he projects to the world of a loving husband and father who works in an upmarket bank and has many working for him. He has a large office, is well dressed and is an upstanding member of society. However, we also see him betraying his family and not really caring about Lola.

In this film we see Lola's strengths as well as her weaknesses. For much of the film we see Lola panicking and screaming to try and release the pressure she is feeling. However, we also see her strength in defending herself. In the second run, after her father slaps her across the face, she destroys his office. She also robs the security officer of his gun and robs the bank in a very calm and determined manner. She knows how to use a gun and she walks out of the bank ready to take the opportunity of not being recognised. Lola is constantly reassuring Manni and never gives up, no matter how close she is to the time deadline.

Lola's vulnerability in her relationship with Manni is evident in the "red scenes". The red light symbolises the passion between Lola and Manni. We witness the genuine love they have for each other as they comment on the pain they would feel if they lost one another. These scenes are significant in portraying their relationship and in building the audience's empathy for them.

## Manni

Manni is an important character in the film. He spends the majority of the film in a phone booth. He has left the bag of money on the train but blames Lola for the fact he had to catch the train in the first place. It is his own past experiences and his consequent paranoia of police officers that result in him fleeing the train, without considering what he was leaving behind.

We do not see Manni's love or concern for Lola in the initial part of the film. He is focused on the belief that he is either going to lose his life or lose his freedom as a result of having to rob a supermarket. His stress and fear are expressed in his interaction with Lola as he desperately yells at her to help him. While Lola tries to be positive and reassuring, Manni finds it difficult to believe that Lola is going to be able to help him. He allows her the chance though, giving her until 12 noon before he takes matters into his own hands and robs the supermarket.

The first time he robs the supermarket he almost gets caught. It is Lola who helps him by hitting the man over the head and knocking him to the floor. In this scene, we see the team work that has developed between Lola and Manni as he pushes the gun back to her to help him finish the job. He clearly values her being there and relies on her or he would not have called her in the

© Five Senses Education Pty Ltd

first place nor wait the twenty minutes for her to try and find a solution to the problem.

It is in the final scenes when Manni is dying that we see his tender side. In the red scenes he discusses with Lola that fact that, if he were to die, she would soon find someone else and she would forget about him. Even though Lola tries to reassure him he is clearly insecure about the situation.

He also shows a soft side when he gets the money back from the homeless man. Despite holding a gun to his head and taking the money he apologises for having to do it. In so doing he shows he has empathy with the homeless man and understands the money would have become important to him. He also trusts the homeless man enough to give him the gun, even though the man could have turned it on Manni immediately and got the money from him. Manni shows that he is actually a decent person who is just in a desperate situation.

The audience is happy that the final scene we witness shows everything working out for Lola and Manni. They walk off happily. Manni has saved the day by getting the money back and so has Lola by winning the money at a Casino. The audience has realised they have great love for each other as their story is told time and time again. The audience want them to end up alive and together at the end!

# THEMES

- Love
- Chance
- Time

## Love

Initially this film may not appear to be a conventional love story, yet the main characters are portraying their own kind of love story. The film opens with them arguing. This reflects their passion. The fear and realisation that Lola may lose Manni if she does not do something to try and save him, becomes apparent.

Manni and Lola are both involved in the crime business. Manni tells Lola they will come after her once they sort him out. It was Lola's responsibility to be waiting for Manni. As her bike got stolen, however, she couldn't be there for him. Manni blames Lola for the money being lost, as he had to catch a train. This is not the safest way to transport money. However, it was because of Manni's past and his previous experience with the law that he panicked and quickly exited the train when he saw police officers. He completely forgot about the money and left it on the train. Manni yells at Lola. She tried to reassure him that she would help him get the money.

For the majority of the film we see Lola desperately running around the streets of Berlin trying to save her lover from being killed. She is so desperate that she screams at her father for help, something that would have been very difficult for her given that they did not have a good relationship. She also robs a bank, putting her own life and freedom at risk in order to save Manni. On another occasion she saves him directly by knocking down a

© Five Senses Education Pty Ltd

security guard and assisting Manni in robbing the supermarket. She continually risks her life and her own freedom to save Manni. In one scene we see Lola accidentally get shot and Manni's reaction to this shows his love for her. Likewise when Manni gets hit by the ambulance, Lola's love and devotion is apparent.

Their love is shown in two key scenes which are both shown while they are dying. These "red scenes" are so named because there is a red light on both of them. The light symbolises their love for each other. Lola and Manni are in an intimate moment and share their deepest feelings for each other. They are in a naked embrace on the bed and are discussing how devastated they would feel if they lost each other. These intimate scenes are important as they foster audience empathy. The audience wants to see the two characters get away with the crime they have committed.

## Time

Time is an important theme in the film. The opening image of the whole film is a clock. It is shown at a low angle so the clock appears larger and the audience recognises the importance of time in this film as even they are dwarfed by it. Throughout the opening credits, an animated Lola can be seen running towards a clock as the sound effects emphasise the ticking sound it is making.

Once we have established the events that are occurring in the film, we realise why time is so important. Manni must get one hundred thousand marks by noon. Lola only has twenty minutes to go until the time deadline runs out. She must see her father, get the money and get back to Manni before he robs the local supermarket. Constant images of clocks are shown throughout the film. They inform the audience how long Lola has left to get to Manni with the money.

Another important aspect of time is that this story is shown in flash forwards and flashbacks rather than chronologically. This means that the audience must constantly piece together the puzzle in order to work out how the characters have arrived at any given point in time. The composers use several techniques such as colour and editing to indicate the passing of time or a flash back for the audience.

Lola and Manni's lives are shown three (different) times over. With each retelling, something has changed slightly which results in Lola or Manni doing things differently. Thus, cause and effect influences the narrative and highlights the importance of timing to the plot.

Lola meets several people on her run who serve to alter the amount of time Lola has left before returning to Manni. For example, the boy on the stairs with his dog trips Lola the second time she is running and consequently slows her down. On this second run she also runs into the woman with the pram and the homeless man. She is slowed down by the fact that her father wouldn't give her the money and so she has to rob the bank. All of these small incidents alter the course of events which affect Lola in some way.

One of the most notable incidents involved Mr Meyer who was picking up Lola's father. The first and second times Lola narrowly escaped getting hit by him. He becomes distracted by her however and consequently hits a white car. This slows him down in picking up Lola's father and consequently Lola is able to see her father

© Five Senses Education Pty Ltd

and witness the affair. In the final scene, Lola lands on the car while the white car drives past. This means Mr Meyer is able to get Lola's father on time and Lola misses out on seeing her father. This works out for the best as Lola goes to the casino and wins the money. However, almost as if it was meant to happen, Mr Meyer still runs into the white car, just at a later point in time.

As a result of alternate scenarios, the importance of timing to the story is foregrounded. This is shown through several techniques. Some have already been mentioned such as the high saturation of images of clocks throughout the film. Another technique is the split screen technique which is an editing tool used by the composers to show several things on the screen at once. In this case, the composers split the screen between Lola, Manni and the town clock to show the struggle between the three of them to make things right. Lola is running to try to get to Manni in time before he walks into the supermarket and robs it. We see in this case, through techniques, that the clock representing time becomes the third most important element in the film after the characters of Lola and Manni.

Re-read the commentary and take note of when the composer uses editing techniques to slow down or speed up time. Usually the speed of the film is slowed to emphasise an aspect of the story.

A close up shot usually reveals the expression on a character's face. If it is a long shot, for example the long, slow shots of Lola running, the audience sees the desperation with which she is running in order to meet her deadline. There are also times when the tempo is sped up for the audience. An example is in the opening scene where people are rushing around. This highlights chaos and action. The audience should be feeling suspense and energy as they watch the action being sped up on the screen.

The opening quotes are also another place where the theme or concept of time is evident. The poet T.S. Eliot reflected deeply on his life and the passage of time. He used many techniques in which he noted time specifically. You may have read some of his poetry in class such as "The Love Poem of J. Alfred Prufrock". *Run Lola Run* opens with a quote by T.S. Eliot which can be interpreted as; "We never give up the search yet, at the end all our seeking we are back at the starting point and will grasp this place for the first time". This quote is highly relevant as it repeats itself three times and continues to move back to the starting point which, in this case, is the telephone receiver falling on the cradle. It is in the last run that Lola seems to "grasp this place" and what she has to do "for the first time". In the film there is a strong suggestion that Lola actually learns from her previous experience.

In the first run she does not know how to use a gun but in the second she seems to have taken the skills she has learnt into the second run of the film. The second quote is from a German soccer coach who is revered in Germany as he led them to a win at the World Cup. Again, the quote plays with the concept of time by stating; "After the game is before the game". In sports terms, the coach could have been commenting that it is the preparation of the team that essentially determines whether they will win and consequently, the game is won or lost before it is even played. This could relate to Lola and Manni as it is the small incidents that determine whether or not they will succeed rather than what they do at the exact moment of noon. You should consider carefully what significance these quotes have for you in your life

© Five Senses Education Pty Ltd

and how you see the experience of time in *Run Lola, Run* as being similar to your life.

There are several aspects to the theme of time. Make sure you consider not just time within the film but also how time is used by the composers to manipulate the audience.


## Chance

This theme is intertwined throughout this text and has been discussed in other areas. It is a very important aspect of the film.

One of the most important scenes where we see chance is in the casino scene in the third run. Lola goes into the casino with minimal money and bets everything she has to try and win enough money to save Manni. Many things in this part of the film are a result of chance. Lola is able to get into the back of the ambulance which means she is able to move quickly. It is a one in a million chance that Lola manages to jump into the ambulance that has someone in it whom she needs to protect and look after. It was her presence that brought the man back from near death. This is emphasised through camera techniques such as the close up shots of the shocked expression on the ambulance driver's face and the close ups of the monitor indicating the patient's remarkable recovery.

The ambulance also, by chance, drops Lola out the front of a casino. We see a long shot of Lola in the foreground and the casino in the background indicating the link between the two. When Lola arrives at the casino, she is told she will not get into the casino, however, she is allowed in. Once inside, Lola puts all of her money on the table and her winnings from the first time.

The chances of winning twice on roulette are very slim, yet Lola manages to do this twice. This indicates that it was fate that dictated Lola was to get the money and save Manni.

There is a very strong suggestion that fate is responsible for our lives. There are many things that stop Lola from getting to Manni with the money and both of them getting out alive in the first two runs. However, Lola was meant to succeed in the third run as all the obstacles that were once there are removed. She seems to only gain advantage and good luck.

## ADDITIONAL RESOURCES

http://www.academia.edu/9581547/RUN_LOLA_RUN_FILM_ANALYSIS

http://germanfilm.co.uk/files/2013/08/Run_Lola_Run.pdf

© Five Senses Education Pty Ltd

# ESSAY QUESTION

Read the question below and then examine the essay outline on the following pages. Use this outline to help guide your planning. Also, try to write a response in other forms other than just essay format. See the end of the sample essay for some other types of formats in which you may be asked to respond.

## QUESTION

*How does the composer use visual techniques to portray the main themes in the film, <u>Run Lola Run</u>.*

# THE ESSAY

The essay has been the subject of numerous texts and you should have the basic form well in hand. As teachers, the point we would emphasise would be to link the paragraphs both to each other and back to your argument (which should directly respond to the question). Of course ensure your argument is logical and sustained.

Make sure you use specific examples and that your quotes are accurate. To ensure that you respond to the question make sure you plan carefully and are sure what relevant point each paragraph is making. It is solid technique to actually 'tie up' each point by explicitly coming back to the question.

When composing an essay the basic conventions of the form are:

- State your argument, outline the points to be addressed and perhaps have a brief definition.

A solid structure for each paragraph is:
- Topic sentence (the main idea and its link to the previous paragraph/ argument)
- Explanation / discussion of the point including links between texts if applicable.
- Detailed evidence (Close textual reference- quotes, incidents and technique discussion.)
- Tie up by restating the point's relevance to argument / question

- Summary of points
- Final sentence that restates your argument

© Five Senses Education Pty Ltd

## As well as this basic structure you will need to focus on:

**Audience** – For the essay the audience must be considered formal unless specifically stated otherwise. Therefore your language must reflect the audience. This gives you the opportunity to use the jargon and vocabulary that you have learnt in English. For the audience ensure your introduction is clear and has impact. Avoid slang or colloquial language including contractions (like doesn't, eg., etc.).

**Purpose** – The purpose of the essay is to answer the question given. The examiner evaluates how well you can make an argument and understand the module's issues and its text(s). An essay is solidly structured so its composer can analyse ideas. This is where you earn marks. It does not retell the story or state the obvious.

**Communication** – Take a few minutes to plan the essay. If you rush into your answer it is almost certain you will not make the most of the brief 40 minutes to show all you know about the question. More likely you will include irrelevant details that do not gain you marks but waste your precious time. Remember an essay is formal so do not do the following: story-tell, list and number points, misquote, use slang or colloquial language, be vague, use non sentences or fail to address the question.

# ESSAY NOTES

**How does the composer use visual techniques to portray the main themes in the film, *Run Lola Run*.**

A few notes about the question:

- It is important to note that you are unlikely to get a question as straight forward as the one above. This will be a good response, however, to help you consolidate your ideas and practise writing.

- Often, the question will have a statement to begin. Make sure you address the statement in your response if you are given one. A good way to do this is to use some of the key words in your topic sentence.

- As there are different types of texts in this module and elective, the question may simply ask you about language. Do not get thrown by this. Remember, your language for this elective is visual language i.e. The language of film. When you see the term language, think visuals, spoken words and voice overs and the meaning shown through them.

© Five Senses Education Pty Ltd

# ESSAY RESPONSE

## How does the composer use visual techniques to portray the main themes in the film, *Run Lola Run*?

The main themes of the film, *Run Lola Run* are time, love and chance. These themes are effectively portrayed through the medium of film and the techniques employed by the director, Tom Twyker. Effective use of visual techniques such as editing, camera shots, angles and symbolism combine to convey the themes.

One of the main themes of *Run Lola Run* is time. This is represented through various techniques. The opening sequence starts with the pendulum of a grandfather clock. The director uses close up shots of the pendulum swinging to indicate that time is of vital importance in this film. The talisman on the end of the pendulum is bright orange. It is presented on a black background so that it stands out as a salient image. After the credits have rolled on the screen, the camera begins to pan up the pendulum and present an extreme, low angle close up of the face of a grandfather clock. This positions the audience submissively in relation to the clock and suggests the power that the clock and consequently, time, will play in the film.

The audience continues to be presented with images of time. Once the animation starts, Lola is seen running down a blue tube-like tunnel with a clock at the end. The audience's first glimpses Lola running towards the clock and time. She often gets sucked up dramatically by the clocks, indicating that she is sometimes powerless against time. Twyker uses editing to highlight the significance of time to the characters during the film.

A split screen shows Manni, Lola and the clock in three equal portions on the screen. Both Lola and Manni are racing against time and Lola tries to get the money to Manni by twelve so he does not have punishment inflicted upon him. This is shown in the film through the split screen technique where the three images are shown to have equal significance in the film. Time is almost personified as a third character in the film, through a high percentage of close up clock face shots. Therefore, through techniques of editing and camera work, the audience is presented with time being a main theme.

Another main theme in the film is love. This theme is shown through camera shots and angles, flash backs and lighting techniques. Manni and Lola, the main characters are in a relationship. The film begins with a very passionate conversation between them where Manni tells Lola that she let him down by not being there to pick him up. Consequently, he has left a bag of money on the train. Lola tries to explain that it was because her moped was stolen. Both are very distressed about the consequences. Lola proves this with a high pitched scream to release her anger. After this scream, the silence is filled with close up shots of Lola's room. One of these close up shots shows a Polaroid picture fixed to the wall. It shows Manni and Lola in an embrace. This indicates to the audience that they are in a relationship. Also, the fact that Manni is calling Lola in his time of crisis shows the bond that they share.

Lola immediately leaves the house to try and save Manni. All of Lola's actions throughout the film show her love for Manni through her determination to get the money for him and possibly save his life. Some of her actions are extreme, such as robbing a bank at knife point and threatening her father. Others are left more to fate such as the incident in the casino. The director uses many

© Five Senses Education Pty Ltd

long shots of Lola running to show her determination to travel to get money and then to get the money to Manni. The action of running shows her distress and her determination. There are also several close up shots of Lola showing the distress on her face and indicating her love for Manni.

After Lola and Manni are shot in the first and second segments of the film respectively, the audience is given a flashback as they are dying. The close up of the dying faces, juxtaposed with flashbacks, indicate that these are the dying thoughts of the characters. Both characters think back to a time when they were together. They talk about how they would feel if they ever lost one another. The camera is at an overhead angle showing the two lovers naked in bed, in intimate conversation. It is a close up shot allowing the audience to see the passionate expressions on their faces. Their placement in each other's arms and their closeness is also highlighted by the close up shot as they fill the whole screen. This could be seen as a metaphor for how they fulfil each other's lives. To add another dimension of meaning, both of these flash backs are filmed with a red light shining on both of the characters. This red symbolises their passion and also danger. Such techniques represent the theme of love and introduce suspense to the audience.

Chance is a theme portrayed in this film. The term chance could also be synonymous with words such as fate and destiny. The editing of this film highlights the major role chance plays in the lives of the characters. The film is three short films in one with each of the three segments representing the same situation being played out in three different ways. Each time, a slight variation on the journey of Lola's run significantly changes the overall outcome, suggesting to the audience the importance of one moment in time and indeed, every moment in time no matter how insignificant it may seem. The audience likewise witness the changing lives of the people who appear on Lola's journey. Their lives have also changed along with Lola's. An example of this is the lady with the pram who Lola runs into as she turns a corner near the beginning of her run. This woman's life changes significantly each time Lola passes by her. In one scenario she becomes a kidnapper after losing her own child to protective services and in another scenario she wins the lottery and becomes wealthy. These flash forwards suggest to the audience that every one is on their own journey. All are subject to the notion that a moment in time can change everything. These flash forwards clearly portray the theme of chance and destiny.

Another significant scene which represent the theme of chance is the casino scene. Everyone in the casino crowds around Lola. Long shots reveal the spectacle she creates in being so lucky. When she leaves, the audience is presented with a long shot of all the people who were in the casino staring blankly after her. This indicates the supernatural and extraordinary nature of what has happened to Lola. It further indicates that this path for Lola has been predetermined. When Lola rolls the dice in the casino we see close up shots of the dice and some of the scene is filmed in slow motion to indicate the gravity of what is happening and to draw the viewer's attention. This also increases suspense for the audience. It is through the technique of editing, through symbolic use of camera shots and angles that the theme of chance is portrayed.

The film director, Tom Twyker, vividly portrays the themes of time, love and chance in **Run Lola Run**. It is through visual

© Five Senses Education Pty Ltd

techniques such as camera shots and angles, editing techniques and symbolism that these themes are so clearly portrayed.

· · · · ·

Now add to this basic essay by taking the approach that visual techniques are underpinned by narrative techniques such as characterisation and setting. By expanding your framework or approach you can show deeper knowledge of the text. Support points with close textual referencing.

# OTHER TYPES OF RESPONSES

**It is crucial students realise that their responses in the examination, class and assessment tasks will NOT always be essays.** This page is designed to give guidance with the different types of responses which may be required.

The response types covered in the exam may include some of the following:

- Writing in a role
- Journal/Diary Entry
- Brochure
- Point of view
- Radio interview
- Television interview
- Letter
- Feature article
- Speech
- Report
- Essay

Students should familiarise themselves with these types of responses and be able to write effectively in them. You should practise each one at some stage of your HSC year.

For a comprehensive explanation of each of these writing forms with examples using the prescribed HSC texts see:

Pattinson, Bruce and Suzan, *Success in HSC Standard English: A Practical Guide for Senior Students*

    © Five Senses Education Pty Ltd

# ANNOTATED RELATED MATERIAL

## Sliding Doors – 1998. Dir Peter Howitt (Film)

This film has very similar themes to *Run Lola Run*. It also highlights the theme of chance and fate. The narrative primarily revolves around how one incident can change the timing of the rest of your life. In this case, the one incident was a woman missing or catching a train. When she caught the train, she came home early to find her partner in bed with another woman. Consequently, she ends a long term relationship and begins a life as an independent woman who finds the challenges of her new found life enable her to find a better life.

However, when she misses the train, the woman is out of her house before she can catch her partner cheating on her and her life continues on as normal and she is miserable.

In the end, the concept of fate is reiterated when her life ends similarly at the end, despite the path she took throughout the film.

Techniques used effectively in this film include editing and camera angles.

## Wicker Park 2004. (Film) Dir Paul McGuigan

This is a romance/horror which also explores the power of fate and destiny, yet in a darker way than *Run Lola Run*.

## Ecclesiastes Chapter 8 verses 1-3

### A Common Destiny for All

1 So I reflected on all this and concluded that the righteous and the wise and what they do are in God's hands, but no one knows whether love or hate awaits them. 2 All share a common destiny—the righteous and the wicked, the good and the bad, [a] the clean and the unclean, those who offer sacrifices and those who do not.

As it is with the good,
so with the sinful;
as it is with those who take oaths,
so with those who are afraid to take them.

3 This is the evil in everything that happens under the sun: The same destiny overtakes all.

This Bible verse reveals the great leveller, Death who will claim us all. According to Christian teachings, there will be a Judgement Day for all,

© Five Senses Education Pty Ltd

# OTHER RELATED MATERIAL

Many of these titles link to post modernism and multiple truths and realities. They tie in with the themes of chance and perspective in your text. *Voices in the Park*, with its multiple perspectives, is more straightforward than some others. The short story is more traditional in its language and written description.

*Alice in Wonderland* - Lewis Carroll/Charles Dodgson (Film and story book)

**Art** - Picasso, Cubism and multiple perspectives, Surrealism - new visual languages. Find specific examples to discuss.

*Cloud Atlas* - Andy and Lana Wachowski, Tom Tykwer (2012 Film)

*Hero* - Zhang Yimou's (2002 Film using multiple perspectives)

*Inception* - Christopher Nolan (Film)

*Memento* - Christopher Nolan (Film)

**Poetry -** Poets use words to create distinctively visual imagery. You could look for descriptive poems about time and fate. Consider 'In the Park' by Gwen Harwood and 'The Glass Jar.' Slessor's poetry also conveys aspects of Time. Alexander Kimmel's didactic poems, " I cannot Forget" contain strong visual imagery. http://remember.org/witness/kimel2

*The Dark Knight* - Christopher Nolan (Film)

*The Gift of the Magi* - O Henry (Short Story). This raises perspective from a more traditional angle through written language. It is poignant in its description and is also based on relationship prompting action.

*The Matrix* - Andy and Lana Wachowski (Film). Postmodern, multiple perspectives of reality.

*The Recognitions* - William Gaddis (Novel) A post modern story organised as a triptych. A challenging read.

*Requiem for a Beast* - Matt Ottley (Picture book)

*Voices in the Park* - Anthony Browne (1999 Picture book). Multiple perspectives, singular event.

© Five Senses Education Pty Ltd

# ACTIVITIES ON RELATED MATERIAL

1. Consider the film *Wicker Park*. As you watch it, identify the film techniques that are used and the main themes of the film. Try to make comparisons with *Run Lola Run* such as the relationships through which the story is told and the techniques that are used to portray similar themes. Also, identify the differences in the two films such as the final outcome and the structure of the text.

   Write one page comparing and contrasting the main themes, the relationships and events through which they are told and the structure of the text. Make sure you are always comparing the visual techniques through which these ideas are conveyed to the audience. Make sure you focus on a few scenes through which you can discuss these techniques clearly. Remember, however, you are best to select a different text type in the exam.

2. Read the bible passage provided for you. What is the message portrayed regarding destiny and fate? Who, according to this passage, is in control of our lives? Who is responsible for deciding our fate? This passage is more about the fateful outcome for humans rather than the journey of fate and the events that happen along the way. How is this different to the messages and themes in *Run Lola Run*?

   Write one page summarizing your ideas. Obviously, this is not a visual text but you can still discuss the techniques that are used to create imagery. Discuss the visual pictures created through written words. Focus on the messages and themes portrayed through this passage.

3. A picture has been provided for you on page 82. Answer the following questions based on the picture.

   a. What is the main theme or idea portrayed in this image? How does it relate to your text?

   b. What comment is being made about that main theme or idea? It is a message of hope, a message of warning or a message to try and motivate people?

   c. Consider the following techniques and comment how they have been used.

   ■ Colour
   ■ Text, if any
   ■ Reader positioning
   ■ Camera angles
   ■ Symbolism
   ■ Image positioning (foreground, background etc)
   ■ Vectors
   ■ Allusion – is there any allusion to another culture or society? What does this suggest about humans taking control of their own fate?

4. Analyse the spoken, written and/or visual language of one related text and evaluate its effectiveness in portraying distinctively visual images for the responder. In your response, select at least three key examples to analyse.

5. After you have completed this task, link your analysis to your prescribed text. Show similarities and/or differences in the language used and the distinctively visual images. (You could link these to setting, theme and/or characters.)

© Five Senses Education Pty Ltd